a gift for

Dad

from

Michael, Jessica

Inspired by the 1950s landmark photographic exhibition, *"The Family of Man,"* M.I.L.K. began as an epic global search to develop a collection of extraordinary and geographically diverse images portraying humanity's Moments of Intimacy, Laughter and Kinship (M.I.L.K.). This search took the form of a photographic competition — probably the biggest, and almost certainly the most ambitious of its kind ever to be conducted. With a world-record prize pool, and renowned Magnum photographer Elliott Erwitt as Chief Judge, the M.I.L.K. competition attracted 17,000 photographers from 164 countries. Three hundred winning images were chosen from the over 40,000 photographs submitted to form the basis of the M.I.L.K. Collection.

The winning photographs were first published as three books titled *Family*, *Friendship* and *Love* in early 2001, and are now featured in a range of products worldwide, in nine languages in more than 20 countries. The M.I.L.K. Collection also forms the basis of an international travelling exhibition.

The M.I.L.K. Collection portrays unforgettable images of human life, from its first fragile moments to its last. They tell us that the rich bond that exists between families and friends is universal. Representing many diverse cultures, the compelling and powerful photographs convey feelings experienced by people around the globe. Transcending borders, the M.I.L.K. imagery reaches across continents to celebrate and reveal the heart of humanity.

www.milkphotos.com

FATHERS

with love

M·I·L·K

MOMENTS INTIMACY LAUGHTER KINSHIP

When a child is born, a father is born.

[FREDERICK BUECHNER]

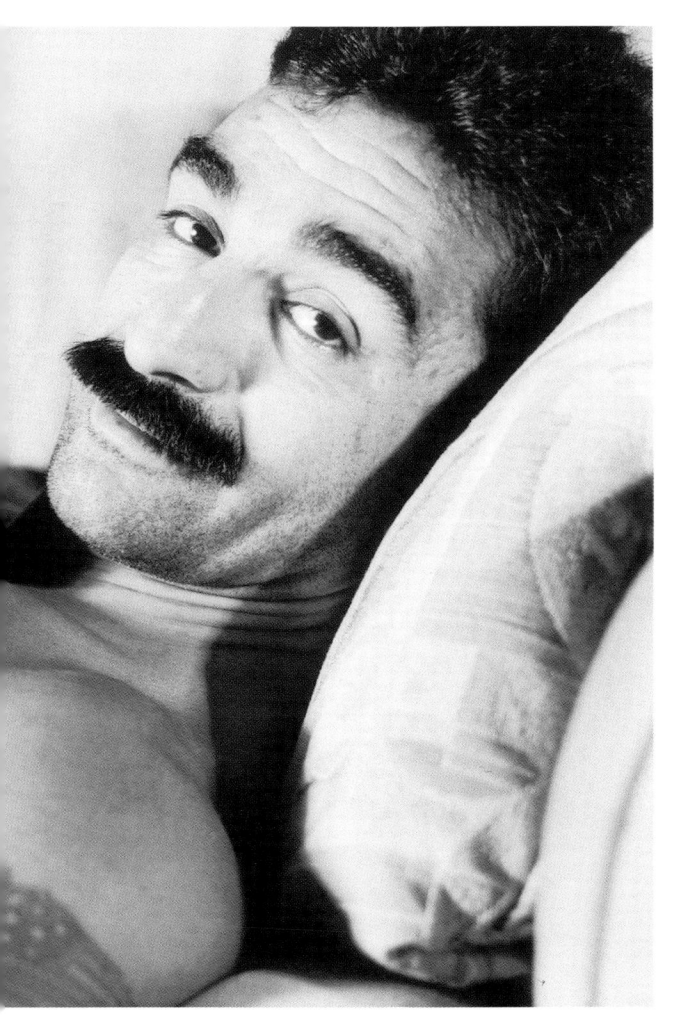

It is not flesh and blood,
but the heart which makes us fathers and sons.

[FRIEDRICH VON SCHILLER]

I do not love him because he is good,
but because he is my... child.

Without a family,
man, alone in the world,
trembles with the cold.

[ANDRE MAUROIS]

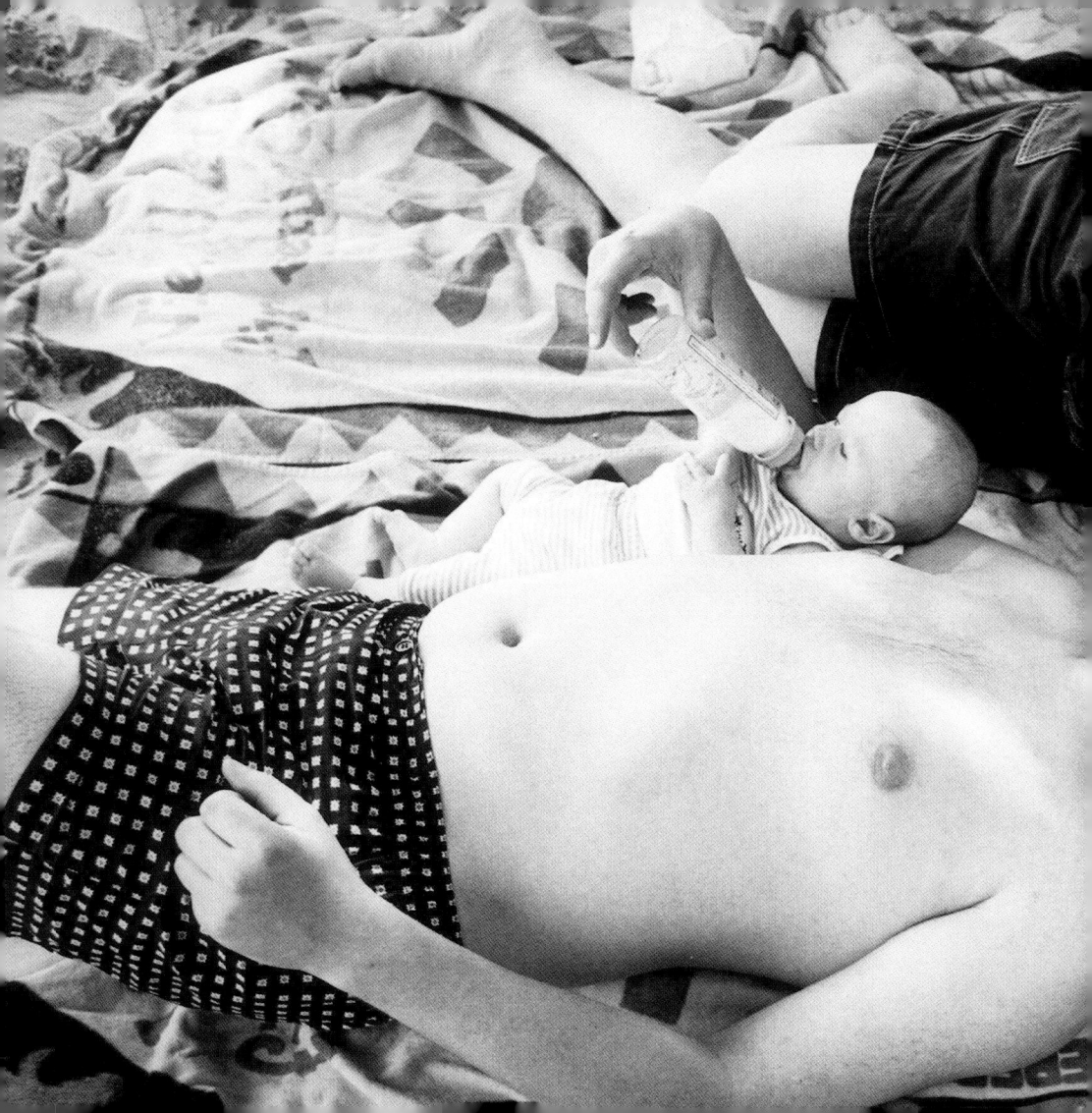

Hold tenderly that which you cherish.

[BOB ALBERTI]

Love is but the discovery
of ourselves in others, and the

delight in the recognition.

[ALEXANDER SMITH]

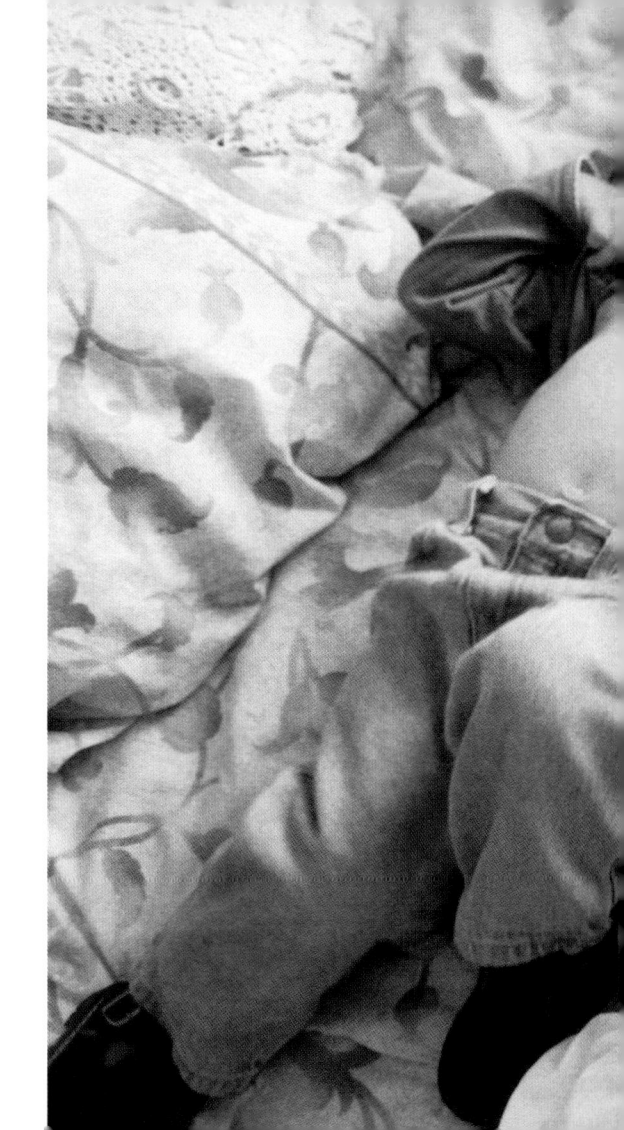

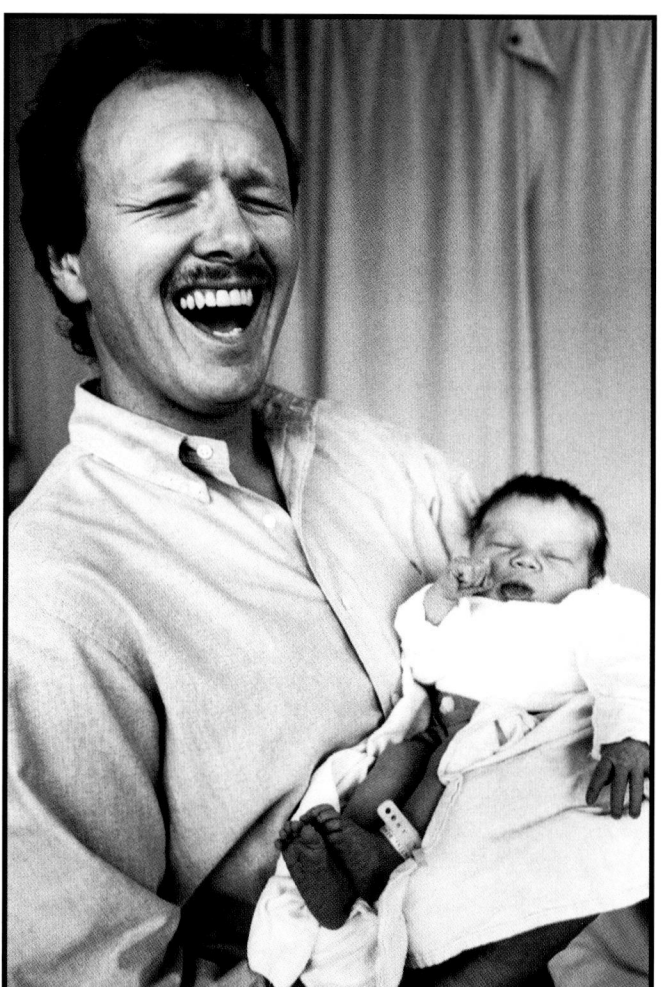

The family is one of
nature's masterpieces.

[GEORGE SANTAYANA]

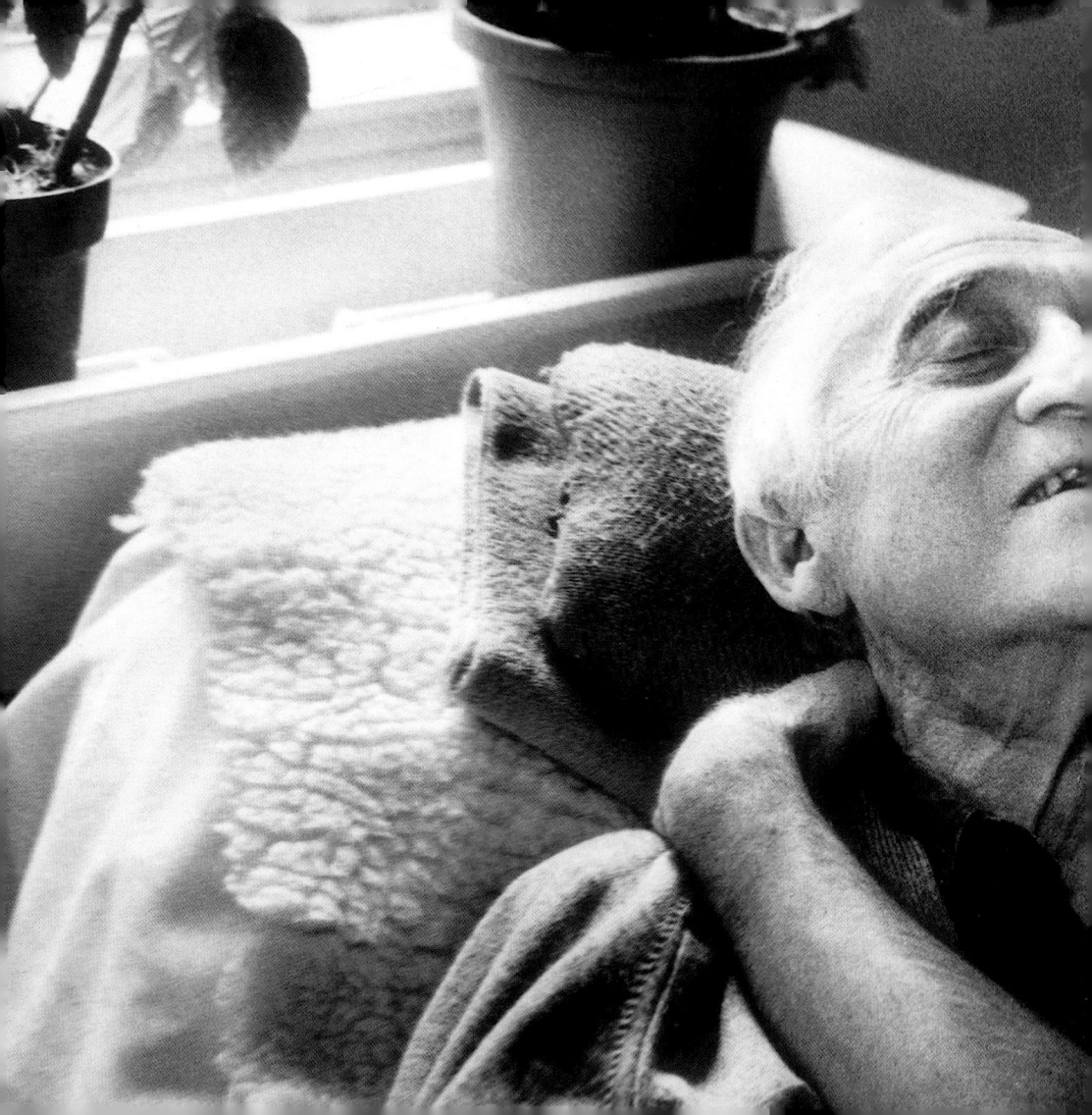

LIVES
WOMEN & MADNESS
OF TWO PEOPLES
MODERN CRISIS
OF THE MIND
and SUBSTANCE

Don't walk in front of me,

I may not follow.

Don't walk behind me,

I may not lead.

Just walk beside me
and be my friend.

[ALBERT CAMUS]

Page 6
© Louise Gubb, South Africa
The simple love of a family bonds a father and son beside the Fiherenana River in Madagascar. The Malagasy people come to this area to mine for sapphires.

Page 8
© Pepe Franco, USA
Father-to-be Angel can't help laughing as he tells a joke to his unborn baby. This image of Angel and his partner, Isabel, was captured during a family party in Aguilas, Spain.

Page 9
© Slim Labidi, France
One-month-old Malik is the centre of attention for his loving parents, Cecile and Hafid, photographed at their home in Villeurbaine, France.

Page 10-11
© Jim Witmer, USA
A photographer father takes a self-portrait with his one-year-old son, Adam, at home in Troy, Ohio, USA.

Pages 12–13
© Henry Hill, USA
Eight-day-old Cyrus is content and secure as he lies sleepily on his father Joe. The young baby had only just left hospital and this image was taken on his first day at home in Colorado Springs, Colorado, USA.

Page 15
© Victor Englebert, USA
In the Amazon rainforest of Brazil, a Yanomami Indian relaxes in a hammock made of bark strips and plays with his young grandson.

Page 16-17
© Jane Wyles, New Zealand
Laughter is infectious for father and son, Drew and James, as they share an affectionate hug in Christchurch, New Zealand.

Pages 18–19
© Kris Allan, UK
Father and son at the Goldstone soccer ground in Hove, England.

Page 21
© John McNamara, USA
The Special Olympics in Union City, California – father Daryl gives his son, JR, a hug full of love and pride after the young competitor finishes his event.

Page 22
© Toshihiro Ogasawara, Japan
Bathtime becomes playtime for Atsuki and his young sons, Yuya, aged one, and Kazuki, three, at the family home in Hyogo, Japan.

Page 23
© Gordon Trice, USA
Father Heath holds his eight-month-old daughter, Bethany. This family portrait was photographed in Abilene, Texas, USA.

Pages 24–25
© Jeremy Rall, USA
A father lifts up his young son to give him a better view of a street festival in Santa Monica, California, USA.

Pages 27
© Maňo Štrauch, Slovak Republic
Outside a Franciscan church in the Slovak Republic, a homeless couple steal a kiss. They are hoping for charitable gifts from the departing congregation. Their three-month-old son, Ivanko, born in an underground cave on the outskirts of the city, yawns as he waits.

Pages 28–29
© Lorenz Kienzle, Germany
A family lies in relaxed contentment on the shore of the River Elbe in Germany.

Pages 30–31
© Martin Rosenthal, Argentina
A father and his children in Juanchaco, Colombia.

Page 32
© Robert Billington, Australia
At the end of the Shark Island swimming race in Sydney, Australia, a one-legged competitor emerges from the surf. His young son hurries over with his artificial limb. This teamwork means his father can run to the finishing line.

Page 33
© Luca Trovato, USA
The Gobi Desert, Mongolia – stranded with all their belongings, a nomadic family are relaxed as they await help.

Page 34
© Marc Rochette, Canada
A look of love and encouragement from father to daughter. Six-year-old Erica's soccer team from Bramalea, Canada, may not win very often, but her father is always on hand to support her efforts in the game.

Pages 36–37
© Dave Marcheterre, Canada
Cheek to cheek – father and daughter hold each other close on a chilly morning in Gaspésie, Quebec, Canada.

Page 38
© Michael Decher, Germany
"Klara and me" – this self-portrait captures a father's face full of tenderness and love as he holds his one-week-old daughter.

Page 39 and back cover image
© Tong Wang, China
A father holds his sleeping child as he cycles through Zhengzhou, China.

Pages 40–41 and front cover image
© Shannon Eckstein, Canada
Rubbing noses in Vancouver, Canada – new father Davy finds the perfect way to bond with his baby daughter, Ciara, only nine days old.

Page 42
© Ray Peek, Australia
"Big" Morrie Dingle, a grazier in South Queensland, Australia, and his two grandsons take a break from the saddle to enjoy some food.

Pages 44–45
© Marcy Appelbaum, USA
In Jacksonville, Florida, USA, two-year-old Rachel is curious to see if her belly button matches her father's.

Page 46
© Marc Rochette, Canada
In Mt Sinai Hospital, Toronto, Canada, new father, Denis, can't contain his delight over new-born daughter, Erica.

Page 47
© Madan Mahatta, India
While his parents visit a camel fair in the desert of Rajasthan, India, a young child enjoys the tender love and care of his grandfather.

Pages 48–49
© Mikhail Evstafiev, Russia
On the streets of Santiago de Cuba, Cuba – a couple's uninhibited display of affection raises a spontaneous smile from their young audience.

Pages 50–51
© Edmond Terakopian, UK
British Royal Air Force sergeant John has just returned from the Gulf War to his wife, Sharon, and their two-year-old son, Phillip. Their reunion was captured during a press conference in Stanmore, Middlesex, England.

Pages 52
© Georgina Lucock, Australia
A quiet moment – parents Kevin and Annette tenderly embrace 10-month-old Jai during a family photo session in Bellingen, Australia.

Pages 54–55
© Stephen Hathaway, UK
Charles and his grandson Richard are deep in conversation as they sit in Soho Square, London, England.

Pages 56–57
© Heather Pillar, Taiwan
Rob Schwartz with his father, Morrie. Mitch Albom, a writer and former student of Morrie, noticed Morrie on a television show and renewed contact with his old professor. The outcome was Albom's moving bestseller *Tuesdays with Morrie*, based on time spent with Morrie on the last 14 Tuesdays of his life.

Page 58-59
© Andrei Jewell, New Zealand
Norbu and his young granddaughter make the most of the warm sunshine in Zanskar in the Indian Himalayas.

What is a Helen Exley Giftbook?

Helen Exley Giftbooks cover the most powerful of all human relationships:
the bonds within families and between friends, and the theme of personal values.
No expense is spared in making sure that each book is as thoughtful and meaningful
a gift as it is possible to create: good to give, good to receive.
You have the results in your hands. If you have loved it — tell others!
There is no power on earth like the word-of-mouth recommendation of friends.

For a full list of Helen Exley's books, write to:
**Helen Exley Giftbooks at 16 Chalk Hill, Watford, WD19 4BG, UK,
or 185 Main Street, Spencer, MA 01562, USA, or visit
www.helenexleygiftbooks.com**

© 2004 PQ Publishers Limited. Published under license from M.I.L.K. Licensing Limited.

All copyrights of the photographic images are owned by the individual photographers
who have granted M.I.L.K. Licensing Limited the right to use them.

First published by Exley Publications Ltd in 2003, 16 Chalk Hill, Watford, Herts, WD19 4BG, UK.

4 6 8 10 12 11 9 7 5

ISBN 1 86187 606 8

Designed by Kylie Nicholls. Printed in China.
Back cover quotation by Frederick Buechner.

MOMENTS INTIMACY LAUGHTER KINSHIP